The Ultimate

GRANADA

Travel Guide

Discovering the Jewel of Andalusia

Alanna Marrow

Table Of Contents

The Ultimate Granada Travel Guide

Map Of Granada

Map data ©2023 Inst. Geogr. Nacional

The Ultimate Granada Travel Guide

Introduction

Step into the enchanting realm of Granada, where centuries of history and culture converge to weave an irresistible tapestry of beauty and wonder. Welcome to the **ultimate Granada Travel Guide,** a comprehensive companion designed to unlock the treasures of this captivating Andalusian gem. Whether you're an intrepid explorer or a curious wanderer, this guide is your key to unlocking the essence of Granada and all it has to offer.

Nestled at the foothills of the majestic Sierra Nevada Mountains, Granada stands as a living testament to its rich Moorish heritage and Spanish legacy. As you turn the pages, you'll delve into the city's past, tracing the footsteps of Nasrid sultans through the resplendent halls of the Alhambra, an architectural marvel that transcends time.

Uncover the secrets of Albayzín, a labyrinthine Moorish quarter, where each cobbled alley whispers tales of ancient civilizations and echoes of flamenco fill the air.

Beyond the historical splendor, Granada's allure lies in its dynamic and vibrant spirit. Traverse the bustling city center, where modernity and tradition harmoniously coexist, and immerse yourself in the lively street markets, the heart of Andalusian charm. Indulge in the art of tapas, where culinary delights await at every turn, inviting you to savor the region's gastronomic treasures.

As you journey through the pages, the guide opens doors to the surrounding wonders of Granada. Explore the Sierra Nevada National Park, a nature lover's paradise offering year-round adventures, from snow-capped peaks to blooming meadows.

Wander through the picturesque villages of Alpujarras, perched like pearls on terraced hillsides, preserving the essence of traditional Andalusian life.

Embrace the warmth and hospitality of the locals, as they welcome you into the heart of their culture, sharing cherished traditions and vibrant festivals that add a special touch to your experience. From flamenco performances that stir the soul to handicrafts that tell stories of skilled artisans, Granada beckons you to become part of its story.

Let this guide be your trusted companion, offering practical travel tips and insider recommendations, guiding you to the hidden gems and unforgettable experiences that make Granada truly unique. Get ready to embark on a transformative journey through time, culture, and nature - an adventure that will forever leave an indelible mark on your heart.

The Ultimate Granada Travel Guide awaits unveiling the secrets of this mesmerizing city, inviting you to create memories that will last a lifetime. Let the journey begin!

Chapter One

About Granada

History

A fascinating story of conquest, cohabitation, and cultural interchange, the history of Granada unfolds like a tapestry. Since ancient times, Granada's destiny has been molded by its strategic location at the meeting point of various civilizations in Andalusia, Spain.

Ancient Beginnings:

The history of Granada dates back to the prehistoric age, and there is proof of human presence reaching back to the Palaeolithic period. Early residents of the area, such as the Iberians and Celts, made their mark, but it was the Phoenicians who first built trading outposts along Spain's southern coast, opening the door for later encounters with other cultures.

Roman and Visigothic Rule:

Later, the Romans took control of the Iberian Peninsula, and Granada, then known as "Illiberis," developed into a significant Roman city. In the area, Roman engineering and architecture are still evident. Visigothic influence briefly appeared after the fall of the Roman Empire, but their authority was short-lived since a fresh force arrived from the other side of the Strait of Gibraltar.

The Moors and the Nasrid Dynasty:

The Islamic religion and Moorish culture were introduced to the Iberian Peninsula with the Umayyad Caliphate of Damascus in 711 CE. Granada flourished under the Nasrid Dynasty and eventually became the final Islamic stronghold in the area. The Alhambra, an exquisite palace-fortress that became the apex of Nasrid architecture, was built under the reigns of Yusuf I and Muhammad V, marking the height of its splendor.

The Reconquista and the Catholic Monarchs:

Granada's collapse marked the end of the Reconquista, a centuries-long effort by Christian nations to retake the Iberian Peninsula. The Islamic era in Spain came to an end in 1492 when Isabella I of Castile and Ferdinand II of Aragon overthrew the city. The Catholic Monarchs were remarkably tolerant of the Moorish inhabitants of Granada despite the conquest, and Islamic traditions, architecture, and customs coexisted peacefully with Christian influence.

The Golden Age of Granada:

Granada enjoyed a golden age of artistic, cultural, and intellectual endeavors while it was ruled by Christians.

The building of the Royal Chapel, which was commissioned to serve as the Catholic Monarchs' final resting place, added to the city's rich architectural history. Science, literature, and the arts experienced a spectacular period of growth during this time, which had a lasting influence on Spain's cultural identity.

Modern Times and the Preservation of Heritage:

The cultural heritage of Granada has developed over the years as a result of influences from many dynasties and cultures. The city saw tremendous urban expansion in the 19th and 20th centuries, although attempts were made to preserve its ancient structures. As a result, the Alhambra and Albayzin were classified as UNESCO World Heritage sites, preserving their relevance for future generations.

Granada is a living example of its lengthy and varied history today. The peaceful coexistence of Islamic, Christian, and modern elements in its energetic streets captivates tourists from all over the world. The fascinating history of Granada serves as a reminder of the enduring legacy of human civilization and highlights the depth of cultural exchange.

Culture

A Melting Pot of Civilizations:

The historical background of Granada, where centuries of Moorish, Jewish, and Christian occupation have left permanent traces, has a significant impact on the city's cultural identity. The elaborate architecture of the Alhambra, where deft arabesques and mesmerizing geometric patterns transport tourists to a bygone era of opulence and artistry, bears tribute to the legacy of Islamic power during the

Nasrid Dynasty. The majestic Cathedral of Granada, which serves as a symbol of religious change and cultural fusion, is also clearly influenced by Christianity.

Flamenco: The Soulful Rhythm of Granada:

Granada is a special place for flamenco, the soul-stirring art style that captures the spirit of Andalusian passion. The rhythmic footwork, eerie tunes, and heartbreaking vocals that fill the city's tablaos (flamenco venues) captivate listeners with their genuine emotion and authenticity. Granada provides a genuine immersion into the heart of this fervent art as it is the birthplace of well-known flamenco performers and musicians.

Gastronomy: A Tantalizing Culinary Adventure:

Due to its distinctive tapas culture, the food scene in Granada is a joy for foodies. Visitors receive a complimentary little plate of delicious snacks with every drink, which encourages them to explore the local cuisine. The regional cuisine tempts taste buds and provides a real sense of Andalusia. Dishes like the famed Sacromonte omelet and savory jamón ibérico are among the region's most well-known dishes.

Festivals and Celebrations:

The city of Granada pulsates with enthusiasm and delight during the city's numerous vivid festivals and celebrations. While the Feria de Corpus Christi celebrates the city's joyous spirit with flamenco dances, fairground attractions, and vibrant parades, the Semana Santa (Holy Week) has serious processions and magnificent floats depicting biblical scenes.

A cultural highlight is the Festival Internacional de Msica y Danza de Granada, which takes place at the Alhambra and features well-known performers from all over the world.

Arts and Handicrafts:

Beyond its ancient landmarks, Granada is a creative powerhouse. Local craftspeople uphold long-standing customs while creating elaborate ceramics, leatherwork, and earthenware that are all embellished with distinctive Andalusian patterns. Visitors can discover tiny workshops where accomplished craftsmen continue to produce works of art that respect the city's aesthetic legacy by exploring Albayzn's winding streets.

Warmth and Hospitality:

The friendliness and hospitality of its citizens form the foundation of Granada's culture. Locals are friendly and willing to share their city's history, customs, and secret attractions with visitors. Travelers feel welcomed guests in this intriguing city thanks to the culture of conviviality and inclusivity, which fosters a sense of belonging.

Geography

The geography of Granada, which is located in southern Spain's Andalusian region, is a mesmerizing fusion of various landscapes and historical sites. The city's unusual location at the foothills of the Sierra Nevada Mountains creates an incredible contrast between the natural splendor and architectural wonders.

With its snow-capped summits, the Sierra Nevada provides Granada with a stunning backdrop and year-round opportunities for outdoor excursions. Winter turns the mountains into a haven for winter sports, drawing skiers and snowboarders from all over. In the warmer months, hikers and nature lovers explore the network of picturesque routes, bringing life to the pristine alpine meadows.

The Alhambra, a famous architectural wonder that crowns the city with its palaces, gardens, and walls, is located in the center of Granada. The breathtaking view of the city and the surrounding surroundings from this UNESCO World Heritage site is evidence of the perfect coexistence of nature and history.

The Albaicn neighborhood, a tangle of winding lanes and whitewashed homes set on a mountainside, adds to Granada's geographic richness. This historic Moorish neighborhood provides breathtaking 360-degree views of the Alhambra and a sense of traveling back in time to the city's first days.

The Genil River softly flows through Granada, dividing it into various neighborhoods and offering both residents and visitors a welcome reprieve.

Chapter Two

Planning your trip

Budgeting (how to save money)

Timing is Everything: Think about going to Granada in the spring or autumn when the weather is nice and there are fewer tourists. Prices for lodging and activities are frequently reduced during these times.

Early Booking: To take advantage of early bird savings and avoid paying higher last-minute rates, make your travel and lodging arrangements well in advance.

Affordable accommodations: Select modest hotels, hostels, or guesthouses in busy areas like the Albayzn or Realejo. Additionally, look into budget-friendly possibilities on websites that provide accommodations and have fantastic offers for longer stays.

Use free attractions and city passes to explore the city's lovely streets and vistas, go on walking tours, and more. Consider getting a Granada Card, which includes local transport and entry to popular attractions like the Alhambra.

Tapas Culture: Enjoy the regional tradition of receiving free tapas at taverns and restaurants with every drink. This is a convenient approach to enjoying delectable food while appreciating the regional flavors.

Picnics & Local Markets: Have a delicious picnic in one of Granada's parks or plazas and splurge on some fresh vegetables and regional delicacies from markets like Mercado San Agustin.

Buses and trams are part of Granada's well-connected public transport network, which you can use to navigate around the city and visit neighboring sites without having to pay for a taxi.

Free Cultural Events: Keep an eye out for free or inexpensive cultural events and festivals, such as musical concerts, art exhibits, and customary celebrations, that will enhance your visit to Granada.

Day Trips on a Budget: Without paying for expensive guided tours, visit neighboring sights like the Sierra Nevada National Park and the Alpujarras towns. You can cut costs by using public transit and self-guided tours.

Travel Passes: If you intend to visit additional Spanish cities, think about getting a Spain Rail Pass or a regional transportation pass, which can save you a lot of money on train and bus travel.

When to visit

The best time to visit Granada will mainly depend on your choices because this wonderful city has its special attractions all year long.

Each season presents a unique view of this Andalusian treasure, from the exuberant celebrations of summer to the warm atmosphere of winter. Here is a schedule to help you determine when to start organizing your trip to Granada:

March to May: Granada is especially lovely in the spring when flowers are in blossom and the weather is pleasant. The grounds of the Alhambra are alive with a riot of color, providing a beautiful backdrop for your journey. You may thoroughly immerse yourself in the historical attractions and take your time exploring Albayzn and Sacromonte's lovely streets because there are fewer tourists than during peak season.

Summertime (June through August)

Granada experiences warmth and a bustling environment during the summer. The length of the days makes it possible to spend more time taking in the sights of the city. However, keep in mind that this is the busiest time of year for tourists, so popular destinations like the Alhambra may become congested and hotel rates may increase. Adopt the siesta as a way of life and take advantage of the nighttime cooling to enjoy tapas and live music in the plazas to beat the heat.

Fall (September through November)

Many tourists prefer the autumn to other seasons to visit Granada. The weather is still great, and when the number of tourists starts to decline, it will be easier to enjoy the city's attractions and exciting festivals. For fans of music, the Granada International Music and Dance Festival takes place in July, while the cooler fall weather is ideal for outdoor pursuits like climbing in the Sierra Nevada or visiting the Alpujarras towns.

December through February is winter.

Granada's winter season has a certain enchantment about it. Winter sports fans have the perfect opportunity to hit the slopes now that the Sierra Nevada is covered in snow. Although it may get colder in the city, the crowded Christmas markets and cozy cafes make it feel cozier. This time of year offers a special perspective on Alhambra, with fewer visitors and a more personal encounter.

How to get to Granada

By Air:

The airport that is nearest to Granada is Federico Garca Lorca Granada-Jaén Airport (GRX), which is located around 15 kilometers from the city center. You can take a taxi, shuttle, or public transportation straight from here to get to Granada.

Some significant airlines provide direct flights to Granada from a few European towns, making it an accessible choice for visitors from abroad.

In a train:

Due to Granada's excellent rail connections, taking the train is a convenient and picturesque option. From towns like Madrid, Barcelona, Seville, and Valencia, frequent connections to Granada are provided by Renfe, the country's rail service. The Granada Estación train station is conveniently situated in the heart of the city, providing quick access to a variety of lodging options and tourist attractions.

By Bus:

Granada is connected to important cities throughout Spain and other parts of Europe by a vast network of long-distance buses. One of the well-known bus companies, ALSA, offers convenient and reasonably priced bus trips to and from Granada.

The major bus terminal in Granada, Estación de Autobuses de Granada, is well situated to allow for simple movement across the city.

By Car:

If you like the freedom of a road vacation, traveling to Granada by car enables you to take your time and take in the breathtaking Andalusia scenery. The A-44 gives access to cities like Jaén and Cordoba, and major motorways like the A-92 connect Granada to places like Seville and Malaga. If you intend to explore Granada on foot, take into account lodgings with parking facilities because parking can be difficult to come by.

Traveling Documents

Passport:

International visitors must have a current passport to enter Spain, including Granada.

To avoid any issues, make sure your passport is valid for at least six months past the dates you intend to go.

Visa:

For stays up to 90 days, citizens of the European Union, the European Economic Area (EEA), and Switzerland are exempt from needing a visa to enter Spain, which includes Granada. However, if you are coming from a nation that needs a Schengen visa, make sure to get it in advance of your trip.

Travel Insurance:

Having travel insurance that covers unexpected events like medical emergencies and trip cancellations is strongly advised, even though it is not a requirement. By doing this, you can travel worry-free and with protection from unforeseen costs.

European Health Insurance Card (EHIC):

Make sure to get the EHIC if you are an EU or EEA citizen so that you can get state-provided healthcare at a discounted rate or occasionally for free during your short stay in Spain.

Evidence of Accommodation:

It is advised to have documentation of your lodging arrangements for the duration of your stay in Granada to satisfy immigration regulations. This can be a letter of invitation if staying with friends or relatives, hotel reservations, Airbnb bookings, or both.

Return or onward tickets:

Your intention to depart Spain before the expiration of your visa or permitted stay may be verified by immigration officials. Make sure you have a return or onward ticket proving you intend to leave the country.

Travel Itinerary and Contact Information:

A thorough travel itinerary with flight information, lodging locations, and scheduled activities might be useful in case there are any questions while you're traveling. Keep the phone number of your embassy or consulate in Spain on hand as well, just in case.

All of your key documents should be copied or digitally copied, and the copies should be kept separate from the originals. To ensure quick access if the physical copies are misplaced or stolen, it is also advisable to store digital copies in cloud storage or email them to yourself.

Local Costumes and Etiquettes of the people

Local costumes: The historical influences on the area can be seen in the traditional Andalusian clothing, which combines aspects from several civilizations.

Even though modern clothing is the norm, you may still see residents at festivals and other important occasions dressed in traditional attire:

For Women: The "traje de gitana" or "flamenco dress," which comes in a variety of hues and patterns and is frequently accessorized with shawls, jewelry, and flower-adorned hairpieces, is the standard attire for ladies. The women's passion for flamenco, a prized art form in Granada, is displayed by their choice of clothing.

For Men: Men may don the "traje corto," a customary short jacket paired with form-fitting pants, which is generally worn for formal occasions or horseback riding.

Etiquettes in Granada:

The people of Granadino are friendly and welcoming, and they appreciate tourists who respect their way of life.

You can interact with people and fully immerse yourself in the culture by being aware of and using the following manners:

Greetings: Accept the Andalusian tradition of warmly greeting others. Both men and women typically shake hands before exchanging two quick kisses on the cheeks with acquaintances and close friends.

Language: Although Spanish is the official language, you may communicate with the locals and demonstrate your interest in their culture by learning a few simple Spanish phrases.

Dining: When eating in neighborhood restaurants, take advantage of the tapas tradition by ordering a drink to receive a free tapa. Before going to the next place, it's traditional to eat tapas in the bar while standing.

Respect for Flamenco: It's important to pay attention and keep silent while watching a flamenco performance. At appropriate times, applaud and express your gratitude to recognize the artists' work.

Siesta Time: Accept the siesta, a noon break when many stores and companies close for a few hours, as a local custom. To respect the inhabitants' sleep, it is a time for relaxing and avoiding loud noises.

Dress code: Even though Granada has a casual dress code, it is appropriate to wear modest clothing when visiting religious sites or going to formal occasions.

Languages spoken in Granada

Spanish (Castilian):

The primary language used in Granada is Spanish. It is used by locals for everyday conversation, business dealings, and encounters with tourists. Your trip experience will be improved and you'll be able to interact with the welcoming locals if you learn a few simple Spanish words.

Andalusian Dialect:

Andalusia is no exception to the rule that each region of Spain has its dialect and accent. The accent, rhythm, and vocabulary of the Andalusian dialect stand out. Talking with the locals might be made more enjoyable by embracing the regional accent.

English:

The main tourist areas in Granada have a high concentration of English speakers and tourists. To service foreign guests, many people employed in the tourism sector, such as hotel personnel, restaurant servers, and tour guides, are fluent in English.

Additional Foreign Languages

You'll come across a wide variety of languages being spoken by both locals and visitors in Granada because it is a well-known tourism destination. As you visit the city's sights and converse with other tourists, you might hear phrases in French, German, Italian, and Chinese.

Arabic:

The history of Granada is intricately entwined with its Moorish past, and Arabic language and culture may still be found today. Even though modern Arabic is not widely spoken, Arabic may yet have influenced some local place names and architectural inscriptions.

University Influence:

One of Spain's oldest and most esteemed universities, located in Granada, draws students from all over the world.

As a result, you can run into pupils speaking in a variety of linguistic environments.

Phrases for Travel

When traveling in Granada, knowing some key phrases in Spanish can go a long way in enhancing your experience and connecting with the friendly locals. While many people in Granada speak English, making an effort to use the local language shows respect for the culture and can lead to more meaningful interactions. Here are some useful phrases to help you navigate your way through this enchanting Andalusian gem:

Basic Greetings:

Hello,: ¡Hola! (OH-lah)

Good morning: ¡Buenos días! (BWAY-nos DEE-as)

Good afternoon/evening: ¡Buenas tardes! (BWAY-nas TAR-des)

Goodnight: ¡Buenas noches! (BWAY-nas NO-chehs)

Goodbye: ¡Adiós! (ah-DEE-ohs)

Polite Expressions:

Please: Por favor (por fah-VOR)

Thank you: Gracias (GRAH-see-ahs)

You're welcome: De nada (day NAH-dah)

Excuse me / Sorry: Perdón / Lo siento (pair-DON / lo see-EN-to)

Asking for Help:

Can you help me, please?: ¿Puede ayudarme, por favor? (PWED-eh ah-yoo-DAR-meh, por fah-VOR?)

Where is...?: ¿Dónde está...? (DOHN-deh eh-STAH...?)

How much is this?: ¿Cuánto cuesta esto? (KWAN-toh KWEH-stah EH-stoh?)

Ordering Food:

I would like...: Quisiera... (kee-see-EH-rah...)

A table for...: Una mesa para... (OO-nah MEH-sah PAH-rah...)

Menu: La carta (lah CAR-tah)

Water: Agua (AH-gwah)

Beer: Cerveza (ser-BEH-sah)

Wine: Vino (VEE-noh)

Bill/check, please: La cuenta, por favor (lah KWEHN-tah, por fah-VOR)

Getting Around:

Where is the bus/train station?: ¿Dónde está la estación de autobuses/trenes? (DOHN-deh eh-STAH lah es-tah-see-ON deh ow-TOH-boo-sehs / tren-es?)

How much is a ticket to...?: ¿Cuánto cuesta un billete a...? (KWAN-toh KWEH-stah oon bee-YEH-teh ah...?)

Where can I find a taxi?: ¿Dónde puedo encontrar un taxi? (DOHN-deh PWEH-doh en-kon-TRAHR oon TA-ksee?)

Emergencies:

Help!: ¡Ayuda! (ah-YOO-dah!)

I need a doctor: Necesito un médico (neh-SEH-see-toh oon MEH-dee-koh)

Call the police: Llame a la policía (YAH-meh ah lah po-lee-SEE-ah)

Chapter Three

Major Cities in Granada

Granada: The provincial capital of Granada is well-known for the Alhambra Palace, an iconic example of Islamic architecture. Granada provides an amazing fusion of Moorish and Spanish elements with a maze of winding lanes in the Albaicn neighborhood.

Almuñécar: This coastal treasure, nestled along the Costa Tropical, enchants tourists with its stunning beaches, verdant scenery, and historic Roman ruins. Both history buffs and those looking to unwind will find it to be the ideal location.

Motril is a significant agricultural and fishing hub known for its lively festivals and energetic environment. Locals and visitors looking for sun and water go to its beaches.

Baza: This city in Granada's north has a rich archaeological history, including prehistoric cave dwellings. It's a distinctive stop on your travel thanks to the bustling markets and old-world charm of Andalusia.

Loja: This calm city is surrounded by breathtaking natural scenery and has historical sites like Alcazaba Castle. There are many chances for outdoor activities given its lovely environment.

Guadix is a city that combines history and modernity. It is known for its cave houses, which offer an amazing look into ancient life.

Best places to visit in Granada

The Alhambra is a magnificent palace complex that is a UNESCO World Heritage site and the crowning achievement of Granada.

It is a must-see because of its exquisite Islamic architecture, gorgeous gardens, and beautiful views of the city.

Generalife Gardens: The Generalife Gardens, which are close to the Alhambra, is an oasis of rich vegetation, fountains, and lovely flowerbeds. These peaceful gardens offer tourists a calm experience that takes them back in time.

Albayzín: Wander through the medieval Moorish district of Albayzn, which is a labyrinth of winding streets and whitewashed homes. The Mirador de San Nicolás provides a picture-perfect vista of the Alhambra against the Sierra Nevada mountains, making this lovely neighborhood ideal for a stroll.

Sacromonte: Granada's ancient past may be seen in a special way in Sacromonte, which is famous for its cave houses.

Discover the region's thriving flamenco scene, with live performances in quaint cave settings.

Cathedral of Granada: Built over more than 180 years, the Cathedral of Granada is a magnificent example of Renaissance architecture. For history and art fans, it is a must-visit location because of its grandeur and extensive interior artwork.

Sierra Nevada National Park: The Sierra Nevada National Park is a playground of rough mountains, deep valleys, and varied fauna for nature enthusiasts and adventure seekers. It's the perfect place to go hiking, skiing, or just to take in the amazing views.

Royal Chapel of Granada: This mausoleum contains the relics of Catholic monarchs Isabella I and Ferdinand II, and it boasts stunning Gothic and Renaissance architecture. The adjacent museum provides information about Spain's royal past.

Monastery of San Jerónimo: This beautiful monastery is a hidden gem that has outstanding Spanish Renaissance architecture and serene cloisters. It offers a tranquil escape from the busy metropolis.

Science Park (Parque de las Ciencias): This interactive museum is great for families and science buffs, with displays on astronomy, physics, biology, and more. For guests of all ages, it is an entertaining and instructive experience.

Transportations

Public Bus: Granada has a sizable bus network that connects a variety of neighborhoods and popular destinations. The buses are reasonably priced and offer a practical way to see the city.

Granada Metro: The metro system in Granada is a cutting-edge addition to the city's transport network. Despite having few routes, it provides a quick and dependable way to move around, especially when traveling to locations outside of the city center.

Taxi: Taxis are easily accessible across the city of Granada and offer a smooth door-to-door travel option. They are especially helpful after hours when public transport may be less common.

Walking and Cycling: Granada is a city that encourages both cycling and walking. For those who prefer cycling, there are designated bike lanes and rental services available, and several attractions are close by.

Train: Granada has a train station with connections to important cities in Spain for longer journeys or to explore nearby cities.

Private Transfers: To conveniently experience the region's cultural and ecological treasures, visitors can also choose private shuttles or guided tours.

Airports

The primary airport in the province, Federico García Lorca Granada-Jaén Airport (IATA: GRX), serves Granada. The airport offers simple access for both domestic and foreign travelers and is situated about 17 kilometers west of the city center. An overview of Federico Garca Lorca Airport is shown below:

1. Connectivity: Federico Garca Lorca Airport provides a respectable selection of domestic and international flights despite being a minor airport. Major Spanish towns including Madrid, Barcelona, and Palma de Mallorca, as well as international locations throughout Europe, are connected for travelers.

2. Terminal Facilities: To ensure that travelers have a comfortable trip, the airport offers modern amenities and services. While waiting for their flights, travelers can unwind and indulge in some shopping or dining at duty-free shops, souvenir shops, restaurants, and cafes.

3. Ground Transportation: There are several ways to go from the airport to the city center. Just outside the terminal, taxis and automobile rental services are easily accessible. Additionally, there are shuttle buses that offer a reasonably priced means to get to many locations in Granada.

4. Accessibility: All passengers, including those with limited mobility, can easily access the airport. It offers services and assistance to make sure that travelers with special needs have a smooth journey.

5. Proximity to Attractions: The Alhambra, Generalife Gardens, and the ancient city center are all within proximity to the Federico Garca Lorca Airport, making it simple for visitors to travel there.

6. Future Developments: To accommodate the growing number of tourists to Granada, there are continuous attempts to upgrade the airport's infrastructure and expand airline options. The airport continues to expand and develop.

The fascinating province of Granada is accessible via the Federico García Lorca Granada-Jaén Airport, which welcomes visitors with its cutting-edge amenities and effective services. The airport offers a smooth and enjoyable start to any journey in this captivating region of Spain, whether travelers are traveling for business or to experience the area's rich cultural legacy and natural beauty.

Taxi

In Granada, taxis are a practical and well-liked method of transportation that give residents and visitors a flexible and hassle-free way to get around the city. What you should know about cabs in Granada is as follows:

Availability: The city center, popular tourist destinations, and transit hubs like the airport and train station are all places in Granada where taxis are readily available. Their striking white color and green stripe make them easy to identify.

Hailing a Taxi: You can call a taxi on the street or at one of the city's approved taxi stands. It's best to go to a taxi stand for faster service during busy hours or in well-known tourist locations.

Taxi Metres: In Granada, taxis have meters that compute the fare based on the amount of time and distance traveled.

To ensure a fair rate, make sure the driver begins the meter at the beginning of your trip.

Tariffs: Taxi rates in Granada are regular, but there may be extra luggage fees, traveling on holidays, or traveling at night. Before setting off on your journey, it is a good idea to inquire with the driver about the approximate fee.

Taxi Apps: Granada taxi companies that offer smartphone apps for booking rides make it simple to call for a taxi and monitor its arrival.

Safety and Reliability: Taxis in Granada are typically secure and subject to strict regulations. The majority of the time, the drivers are kind and educated about the city's attractions, providing tourists with helpful advice.

Shared taxis: In Granada, there are "colectivos"—shared taxis—that go along predetermined routes and accommodate many passengers. These shared taxis are a more affordable choice for quick city trips.

Car Rentals

Rental Agencies: The Federico Garca Lorca Granada-Jaén Airport and the city center both have a wide selection of renowned automobile rental companies. Major international brands and regional businesses offer a selection of vehicles to fit various spending limits and preferences.

Booking in Advance: Especially during the busiest travel seasons, it is advised to reserve your vehicle hire in advance to lock in the best deals and guarantee availability.

Requirements: You normally need to be at least 21 years old (age requirements may vary by company) and have a valid driver's license to rent a car in Granada.

In addition to their home country's license, foreign tourists may also need an International Driving Permit (IDP).

Insurance: To cover any accidents or damages, car rental companies provide a variety of insurance choices, such as Collision Damage Waiver (CDW) and Theft Protection. It's crucial to comprehend the insurance policies and, if necessary, to look into supplemental coverage.

Traffic and parking: It's important to obey all traffic regulations and road signs when driving in Granada. It is advised to use public parking lots or garages because parking in the ancient city center can be difficult due to the small streets.

Exploring the Region: With a rental car, you can travel outside of Granada to discover the breathtaking countryside, which includes the Sierra Nevada mountains, charming villages, and other local attractions.

GPS and maps: Car rental companies frequently provide GPS navigational devices, or you can utilize smartphone apps. A real map is also useful to have on hand, especially when visiting off-the-beaten-path locations.

Fuel: There are several petrol stations in Granada, and most of them accept payments with major credit cards. Think carefully about refueling the automobile before returning it because some rental firms demand that you return it with a full tank of petrol.

Chapter Four

Accommodations

Resorts and Hotels

Luxury Resorts: Granada is home to some opulent resorts that provide top-notch services and stunning vistas for visitors looking for the best indulgence. These resorts frequently have opulent spas, fine dining establishments, and magnificent rooms with breathtaking views of the countryside.

Historic Hotels: Granada's historic hotels, many of which are housed in exquisitely restored structures with elaborate architecture and distinctive charm, represent the city's rich history. While enjoying contemporary conveniences, staying at these hotels offers a window into the city's past.

Boutique Hotels: Numerous boutique hotels in Granada provide visitors with a unique and private experience. These accommodations are perfect for guests seeking a more distinctive stay because of their chic interior design, meticulous attention to detail, and welcoming atmosphere.

City Center Accommodations: Granada's city center is littered with a range of hotels, from moderately priced properties to five-star establishments. Staying in the city center gives you quick access to popular sights, shopping areas, and buzzing nightlife.

Accommodations near Alhambra: Some hotels and resorts are ideally situated close to the renowned Alhambra Palace, providing mesmerizing views of this UNESCO World Heritage site. Visitors eager to explore the historic landmark greatly prize these accommodations.

Rustic Retreats: There are quaint country hotels and rustic retreats on the outskirts of Granada. These homes provide a peaceful haven amid stunning surroundings and a classic Spanish feel.

Family-Friendly Hotels: Many hotels in Granada offer rooms that are roomy, kid-friendly amenities, and activities appropriate for kids of all ages.

Budget Accommodations: Budget lodging options include hostels, guesthouses, and reasonably priced hotels that provide comfortable stays without breaking the bank. These inexpensive lodging options may be found all across the city and provide visitors with a practical choice.

Eco-friendly lodging: Granada is also home to environmentally responsible hotels and resorts that place a high priority on sustainability.

For visitors who care about the environment, these businesses provide ecologically friendly amenities and procedures.

Camping Sites

Sierra Nevada National Park: Adventure seekers frequently choose to camp in the Sierra Nevada. The park has some primitive campsites that let visitors enjoy the spectacular mountain landscape and outdoor pursuits including hiking, rock climbing, and birdwatching.

Alpujarra Region: The Alpujarra region, which is sandwiched between the Sierra Nevada and the Mediterranean Sea, has attractive campgrounds that offer a tranquil and relaxing camping experience. It's the perfect place to relax and get in touch with nature, surrounded by terraced fields, white-washed villages, and natural springs.

Camping by the Lakes: The picturesque reservoirs of Canales and Bermejales, which are close to the city of Granada, are surrounded by camping areas. These areas give campers the ability to take part in water sports like swimming, fishing, and canoeing while being surrounded by beautiful scenery.

Sierra de Baza Natural Park: The Sierra de Baza Natural Park is a beautiful camping location with a variety of flora and fauna. The park has some well-equipped campsites that serve as a great starting point for exploring its breathtaking trails and taking in the local fauna.

Coastal camping: There are campgrounds near the beaches along the Costa Tropical of Granada where guests can take in the sun, sea, and sand. Camping near the ocean gives a revitalizing coastal experience with a wide range of water sports and beach pursuits.

Natural Retreats: Some camping grounds in Granada provide a more secluded and natural escape away from the busy tourist regions. These remote areas are ideal for people looking for peace and a chance to escape the hectic pace of modern life.

Chapter Five

Exploring Surrounding Areas

Day Trips from Granada

Alhambra & Generalife Gardens: While visiting Granada, you must pay a visit to the Alhambra Palace, which is renowned, and its breathtaking Generalife Gardens. Discover the interesting history, lush gardens, and exquisite Islamic architecture at this UNESCO World Heritage site.

Sierra Nevada Mountains: A day excursion to the Sierra Nevada, Spain's tallest mountain range, will be a treat for nature enthusiasts. Enjoy outdoor pursuits like skiing or hiking while soaking in the mesmerizing vistas of the nearby valleys.

Alpujarra Region: Visit the charming Alpujarra settlements, which are nestled on the southern slopes of the Sierra Nevada. Learn about the welcoming folks, historic architecture, and quaint white-washed villages.

Salobreña: Visit the beach town of Salobreña by traveling to the Costa Tropical. Enjoy its stunning beaches, tour the medieval castle, and indulge in mouthwatering seafood cuisine.

Nerja: A breathtaking coastal town famous for its breathtaking Balcony of Europe viewpoint, magnificent caverns, and white sand beaches.

Ronda: Despite being a more time-consuming day trip, Ronda is worthwhile due to its magnificent cliffside environment, historic bridges, and rich culture.

Cordoba: A renowned example of the fusion of Islamic and Christian architecture is the Mezquita Cathedral in Cordoba, which can be reached from Granada by high-speed train.

Malaga: Enjoy a day of exploration in Picasso's birthplace, Malaga, a bustling city with cultural attractions, a lively atmosphere, and stunning Mediterranean beaches.

Sierra Nevada National Park

In the Spanish province of Granada, Sierra Nevada National Park is a spectacular natural wonder that mesmerizes tourists with its imposing mountains, varied landscapes, and teeming animals. An overview of the breathtaking Sierra Nevada National Park is provided below:

Mountain splendor: Mulhacén, the tallest peak in mainland Spain at 3,479 meters above sea level, is located in the Sierra Nevada. The park's snow-capped summits are a sanctuary for hikers and mountaineers and make a magnificent contrast to the clear skies.

Outdoor Activities & Hiking: The park has a network of clearly marked hiking routes for hikers of all skill levels. Outdoor enthusiasts have a wide range of options, from relaxing strolls across beautiful meadows to strenuous climbs up mountain slopes.

Skiing & Winter Sports: Sierra Nevada, one of Europe's most southern ski resorts, transforms into a winter wonderland throughout the winter months. Modern facilities and exceptional snow conditions are available for skiers and snowboarders.

Biodiversity: Sierra Nevada National Park was designated a UNESCO Biosphere Reserve for its exceptional biodiversity. Many different plant and animal species, some of which are unique to this area, are supported by its various habitats.

Flora and fauna: A diversity of flora, such as historic yew forests, fragrant lavender fields, and indigenous plants, can be seen by visitors. The park is a haven for birdwatchers as it is also home to the elusive Spanish ibex, golden eagles, and numerous bird species.

Stargazing: Because of its extremely clear sky, Sierra Nevada has been classified as a Starlight Reserve. The park provides an exceptional opportunity for stargazing on clear nights when the Milky Way and myriad constellations brighten the night sky.

Cultural Heritage: The park is rich in history and has ruins of Moorish architecture as well as historic mountain communities and historical settlements.

The Alpujarras Villages

The Alpujarra region near Granada, Spain, is a collection of lovely white-washed towns that radiate tranquility and timelessness. It is situated on the southern slopes of the Sierra Nevada mountains. A peek at the charming Alpujarras settlements is shown here:

Traditional Architecture: The whitewashed, flat-roofed towns in the Alpujarras region exhibit a distinctive architectural style that hasn't evolved much through the years. The communities seem to mix in seamlessly with the natural surroundings, making for an alluring sight.

Bubión: This adorable village has meandering, crooked alleyways lined with bright flower pots and typical Alpujarran structures. Bubión is a haven for nature enthusiasts and photographers because of its breathtaking views of the Poqueira Gorge and the huge lowlands below.

Pampaneira: One of the most well-liked towns in the Alpujarras, Pampaneira is renowned for its lively vibe, artisan stores, and craft studios. Shoppers will get delectable regional delights as well as handmade handicrafts like textiles and ceramics.

Capileira is the tallest town in the Poqueira Valley, perched at a lofty 1,436 meters above sea level. It makes a great starting place for hiking trips because of its terraced streets, which offer panoramic views of the majestic mountains.

Trevélez: At 1,476 meters above sea level and well known for its jamón serrano (cured ham), Trevélez is the highest hamlet in Spain. In addition to savoring the regional cuisine, tourists may take in the village's distinctive architecture and rustic way of life.

Órgiva: Órgiva, one of the bigger communities in the Alpujarras, offers a blend of contemporary conveniences and classic charm. It is a perfect home base for touring the area because it is surrounded by lush orchards and productive agriculture.

Soportújar: A lesser-known gem, Soportjar is a secluded community that provides a tranquil refuge from the busier tourist areas. It's a hidden paradise in the Alpujarras due to its serene surroundings and close contact with nature.

Costa Tropical and Beaches

Costa Tropical, a sun-kissed paradise offering a lovely fusion of Mediterranean coastline and lush tropical scenery, is situated in the province of Granada, Spain. Here's a snapshot of Costa Tropical's splendor and its alluring beaches:

Coastal Beauty: Costa Tropical, which spans along the Mediterranean Sea, is known for its beautiful beaches and pristine waters. The coastline is distinguished by its distinctive microclimate, which enhances the attraction of the area by enabling the development of tropical fruits like mangoes, avocados, and bananas.

Playa de la Herradura is a well-liked vacation spot for both locals and tourists. It is a horseshoe-shaped beach. It's a picture-perfect location for swimming, snorkeling, or just lazing in the sun thanks to its quiet waters and beautiful pebble coastlines.

Playa de Velilla: Playa de Velilla provides a laid-back and welcoming ambiance with its palm-lined promenade and beautiful sands. The beach is convenient for a day of beachfront enjoyment because it is well-equipped with amenities.

Playa de Cantarriján is a quiet, nudist-friendly beach that is encircled by rocks and vegetation. It is located inside a protected natural park. It's the ideal location for people looking for peace and a sense of connection to nature.

Watersports Haven: Costa Tropical's tranquil waters and moderate winds make it the perfect location for lovers of water sports. Along the coast, visitors can engage in activities like sailing, paddleboarding, and kayaking.

Charming Coastal Towns: The area is peppered with little coastal towns like Almuécar and Salobrea, each of which offers a distinctive blend of history, culture, and seaside appeal. Visit their historical sites, stroll through their charming streets, and indulge in the excellent seafood served at their seaside eateries.

Subtropical Climate: Costa Tropical enjoys a moderate subtropical temperature that makes it a year-round travel destination. The winters are delightfully warm, while the long, bright days in the summer are ideal for beach excursions.

Scenic Drives: Costa Tropical's coastal roads offer stunning views of the Mediterranean Sea and the neighboring mountains to drivers.

Chapter Five

Sightseeing

Ancient Monuments

Alhambra Palace: The magnificent 13th-century palace complex known as the Alhambra is the jewel in the crown of Granada's historic sites. The Alhambra is a UNESCO World Heritage site and a must-see for everyone traveling through Granada because of its exquisite Islamic architecture, gorgeous courtyards, and elaborate tilework.

Generalife Gardens: The Generalife Gardens, which are close to the Alhambra, are an outstanding example of Islamic landscaping. These rich gardens offer a tranquil retreat from the busy city and contain lovely fountains, pavilions, and elegant walks.

Granada Cathedral is a magnificent structure that represents Renaissance architecture and took more than 180 years to finish. Magnificent altars, holy artifacts, and breathtaking artwork are housed within its opulent interiors and imposing exterior.

The **Royal Chapel of Granada** is a mausoleum that houses the remains of Catholic monarchs Isabella I and Ferdinand II. The chapel's spectacular Gothic and Renaissance design makes it an important historical site. It is located near to Granada Cathedral.

The **Albaicín Quarter** is a well-preserved old neighborhood with meandering streets, traditional buildings, and Moorish architecture, despite the absence of any monuments. This historical region provides fascinating views of the Alhambra and a window into Granada's past.

Corral del Carbón: Corral del Carbón is a Moorish-era structure and one of the oldest in Granada. It has a beautiful Islamic design and serves as a reminder of Granada's commercial past as a coal and grain exchange and caravanserai.

The **Madrasah of Granada** provides a reminder of the city's Moorish past, although being only partially intact. The elaborate calligraphy and stucco work in this old Islamic school reflect the period's creative and intellectual achievements.

Museums

The Alhambra Museum, which is housed within the Alhambra Palace complex, exhibits artifacts and historical items connected to the Alhambra's past. The Nasrid dynasty, Islamic art, and the palace's development over the years are all topics that tourists can learn about.

Granada Fine Arts Museum (Museo de Bellas Artes de Granada): Spanish art from the 15th to the 20th century is on display in the Granada Fine Arts Museum (Museo de Bellas Artes de Granada), which is housed in a former palace from the 16th century. It features pieces by well-known artists like Diego Velázquez, Francisco de Goya, and Alonso Cano.

The **Museum of Archaeology of Granada (Museo Arqueológico de Granada)** explores the history of Granada by displaying artifacts from prehistoric to Islamic eras. It provides a window into the various historical periods of the area.

The **Science Park (Parque de las Ciencias)** is a fun-filled, family-friendly museum that features interactive displays on a range of scientific topics, from biology to astronomy. All ages can learn and explore in this interesting environment.

San Juan de Dios Museum: The Basilica of San Juan de Dios houses the San Juan de Dios Museum, which pays homage to St. John of God, a key figure in the history of Granada. It displays works of religious art, artifacts from history, and the saint's personal effects.

Federico García Lorca House-Museum: The famous poet Federico Garca Lorca is the subject of this museum, which is housed at Huerta de San Vicente, the home where he spent his summers. It provides a look at the poet's life, his creative output, and his enduring impact on Spanish literature.

Casa de los Tiros: This museum showcases a varied collection of artwork, ceramics, costumes, and historical artifacts and concentrates on the history and customs of Granada.

The **Manuel de Falla Museum** is a memorial to the well-known composer Manuel de Falla that houses a collection of artifacts, musical scores, and personal items.

Shopping

Alcaicería Market is a historic market that dates back to the Nasrid era and is close to the Cathedral. It was formerly a lively silk market, but it is now home to a colorful collection of stores selling traditional Andalusian goods, handicrafts, souvenirs, and spices.

Puerta Real: With its abundance of shops, boutiques, and department stores, this busy thoroughfare in the center of Granada is a shopper's paradise. From Spanish and international companies, you may find contemporary products, accessories, and clothing here.

Albayzín District:: Artisan studios and specialty shops providing handcrafted leather, textiles, and ceramics are strewn throughout the cobblestone alleyways of Albayzn. It's the ideal location for discovering distinctive and genuine souvenirs.

Centro Comercial Neptuno: This shopping center in the heart of the city offers a contemporary shopping experience. There are several different types of stores there, including electronics stores, apparel stores, and a sizable supermarket.

Paseo de los Tristes: You may find quaint boutiques and artisanal businesses selling handcrafted goods, jewelry, and artwork along the charming Paseo de los Tristes.

Street Markets: On particular days of the week, Granada organizes many street markets that sell fresh food, flowers, clothing, and antiques.

The second-hand merchandise and antique finds at the Mercado de San Agustn are especially well-liked.

El Corte Inglés is a well-known Spanish department store with a large assortment of goods, including fashion, electronics, and gourmet food items. It is situated in the heart of the city.

Tapas Souvenir: Don't pass up the chance to bring home a "tapa" souvenir—a distinctive custom in Granada where drinks are served with complementary little plates of food. Many tapas bars provide vibrant ceramic plates or glasses, which make for a lovely and useful souvenir.

Chapter Six

Outdoor Activities

Hiking and Nature Walks

Sierra Nevada National Park: The Sierra Nevada mountains offer an abundance of hiking trails that are appropriate for hikers of all skill levels. The park's varied terrain accommodates a range of preferences and fitness levels, offering everything from easy nature hikes through pine forests to strenuous ascents up the summits.

Alpujarras: The gorgeous Alpujarra region offers a network of trails that weave past terraced fields, luscious orchards, and traditional farms. It is known for its attractive white-washed villages. The neighboring valleys and mountains can be seen in exquisite detail from the beautiful pathways.

Los Cahorros: The Monachil Valley's Los Cahorros is a well-liked trekking area known for its hanging bridges, constricting gorges, and breathtaking waterfalls. For those who enjoy the outdoors and exploring nature, the trail offers a thrilling experience.

Cumbres Verdes: Granada's neighbor, the Cumbres Verdes, is home to many clearly defined hiking trails that wind through pine forests and along ridges. It's a great place to observe birds and take in the peace of nature.

Río Darro Walk: The Ro Darro Walk traverses the old districts of Granada as the Darro River winds its way through the city. It provides lovely views of the Alhambra and the wonderful architecture of the city.

Vereda de la Estrella: Vereda de la Estrella is a strenuous but rewarding walk that takes you through stunning scenery like streams, meadows, and high mountain regions.

The Mulhacén, mainland Spain's highest mountain, is visible from the trail's apex in breathtaking views.

Cerro del Sol: A relatively short walk that offers panoramic views over the city and the surrounding Vega de Granada is Cerro del Sol, which is located on the outskirts of Granada.

Quentar Reservoir: The Quentar Reservoir, which is a part of the Sierra de Huétor Natural Park, offers a serene location for a stroll while surrounded by stunning scenery and chances for birdwatching.

Skiing and Winter Sports

Skiing in the Sierra Nevada: As one of Europe's most southern ski resorts, Sierra Nevada is a distinctive and popular destination for winter sports aficionados. With more than 100 kilometers of skiable terrain and great snow from December to April, Sierra Nevada provides skiers of all skill levels with an unforgettable skiing experience.

Snowboarding: The resort offers exhilarating freestyle zones and specific snow parks for snowboarders. It is a favorite location for snowboarders because of the varied terrain and well-kept facilities.

Winter Hiking: The Sierra Nevada mountains also provide stunning winter hiking trails in addition to skiing and snowboarding. As you walk the trails, take in the refreshing mountain air and the breathtakingly beautiful snowy scenery.

Cross-Country Skiing: Sierra Nevada offers cross-country skiing alternatives, allowing you to glide along designated tracks and take in the serene winter environment.

Snowshoeing: Try snowshoeing in the unspoiled environment of the Sierra Nevada for a singular and peaceful winter experience.

It's a great opportunity to experience nature up close and discover regions that are inaccessible to regular skiing.

Apres-Ski: Granada's thriving apres-ski scene is waiting for you after a day on the slopes. There are many bars, restaurants, and places to go out and have fun in the ski resort and the adjacent towns.

Ski Schools and Equipment Rental: The ski resort has top-notch ski schools and instructors to help you, whether you're a beginner or trying to hone your abilities. For individuals who would rather not bring their gear, equipment rental services are also available.

Accessibility: The city center of Granada is close to the Sierra Nevada ski resort, making it ideal for day visits or overnight stays.

Rock Climbing and Adventure Sports

The magnificent Sierra Nevada Mountains will capture the attention of rock climbers. The area offers a variety of climbing routes for climbers of all skill levels, from easy walls to difficult crags. Those that scale these difficult heights will be rewarded with breathtaking sights and a sense of achievement.

For those seeking adventure, Granada also offers a wide variety of adventure sports. Explore the area's varied topography and historic paths by setting off on spectacular mountain bike tracks. Paragliding is an exciting activity that thrill-seekers may partake in to soar through the air while taking in Granada's breathtaking views from a different angle.

The neighboring rivers and reservoirs provide kayaking and canoeing opportunities for water sports lovers. The region's pleasant Mediterranean climate makes it possible to take advantage of outdoor activities all year round.

In addition to the sense of excitement, Granada provides a rich cultural experience. Visitors can take in the Moorish architecture, tour the historic Alhambra palace, and sample regional cuisine at quaint cafes.

Chapter Seven

Food and Drinks

Restaurants

The streets are lined with tempting tapas bars that tempt tourists with a variety of tasty small plates. In Granada, where the tapas tradition is prominent, ordering a drink frequently includes a complimentary tapa, allowing customers to indulge in a range of regional specialties.

Restaurants provide delectable fare including paella, gazpacho, and tender grilled meats for customers seeking authentic Spanish food. A genuine flavor that evokes the spirit of Granada's culinary tradition is ensured through the use of locally obtained products.

Granada's international eating scene is equally spectacular as its Spanish dining scene.

Without leaving the city, guests can travel the world through food by dining at Middle Eastern and Italian trattorias.

Granada offers a fantastic assortment of wines from the adjacent Andalusian region vineyards to go along with the delectable cuisine. The wine selection, whether it's a deep Rioja or a fresh Albario, will improve the meal experience. The stunning scenery of numerous restaurants adds to the allure of dining in Granada. These restaurants' settings make for unforgettable and romantic dining experiences, whether they are tucked away in little cobblestone alleys, positioned on hilltops with breathtaking views, or hidden within medieval courtyards.

Local cuisine

"Tortilla del Sacromonte," a distinctive omelet created with soft bits of pork, savory herbs, and a medley of vegetables, is one famous dish that perfectly encapsulates the essence of Granada's cuisine. "Habas con Jamón," a delicious dish of fresh broad beans sautéed in garlic and olive oil and then topped with salty Spanish cured ham, is another regional specialty that you simply must taste.

Due to Granada's proximity to the Mediterranean Sea, there is no shortage of delicious seafood. Prawns cooked in sizzling olive oil, garlic, and chili are known as "Gambas al Pil Pil," and both residents and tourists adore them. The "Calamar a la Romana" is a delicious tapas meal that comprises succulent squid rings covered in a light and crispy batter.

"Plato Alpujarreo" is a divine option for carnivores. Blood sausage, cured gammon, eggs, and potatoes are all combined in this filling dish to create a savory symphony. A genuine treat for the senses, "Cordero a la

Miel," soft lamb cooked with honey and spices, exemplifies the Moorish traditions of the area.

Granada offers a variety of regional wines and cooling beverages to go along with the assortment of cuisine. The rich and varied flavors of the regional food go nicely with a glass of "Vino de la Tierra," a local wine.

Local Drinks

"Tinto de Verano," which translates to "Summer Red Wine," is a popular local beverage that epitomizes Granada. It is a straightforward but tasty combination of red wine and carbonated lemonade, served over ice. It's a well-liked option among both locals and visitors alike and is ideal for warm days.

Another well-liked local favorite is the artisan beer "Cerveza Alhambra," which gets its name from the illustrious Alhambra palace.

This beer, which comes in a variety of varieties and is brewed with premium ingredients and a strong sense of heritage, works incredibly well with the tapas culture of the city.

"Granadino Horchata" is a delicious option for individuals looking for a non-alcoholic beverage. This sweet and creamy beverage, which is made from tiger nuts, water, and sugar, offers a refreshing break, especially during the sweltering summer months.

"Ponche Segoviano" is a dish that must be tried if you want to get a flavor of the area's history. This age-old liqueur, made by combining aniseed, brandy, and sweet syrup, is smooth and aromatic and has been enjoyed for generations.

Moroccan tea, also known as "Té Moruno," is a popular choice for a taste of the unusual.

It provides a distinctive and refreshing experience with North African characteristics thanks to its combination of green tea, mint, and sugar.

Street foods

The "Bocadillo de Calamares" is one of Granada's most recognizable and well-loved street snacks. This mouthwatering sandwich consists of tender rings of crispy fried squid wrapped within a soft baguette, providing a savory and filling lunch that is ideal for wandering around the city's gorgeous streets.

"Churros con Chocolate" is a must-try for individuals who are in the mood for a quick and flavorful snack. Traditionally, a cup of thick, rich chocolate is used to dip these sugar-dusted, fried dough pastries. This comfort food is especially well-liked during the cooler months.

The vivacious markets of Granada are a veritable foodie paradise. Locals love the dish "Pescadito Frito," which is fried fish served on tiny wooden skewers. It delivers a taste of the Mediterranean Sea in every crispy bite since it is freshly caught and well seasoned.

The "Montadito de Pringá," a little sandwich stuffed with soft, slowly-cooked pork, chorizo, and morcilla (blood sausage), is another market favorite. This hearty snack is a fantastic representative of the local cuisine and is bursting with strong flavors.

"Granizado de Limón" is a tasty option for quenching your thirst. On hot summer days, this cold lemon slush is the ideal way to stay cool while getting a lemony boost.

Chapter Seven

Safety and Health

Vaccinations

Check your current status about routine vaccinations before traveling anyplace. Measles, mumps, rubella, diphtheria, tetanus, pertussis, and influenza vaccines are possible among them.

Hepatitis A vaccination is strongly advised for visitors to Granada, particularly if they intend to sample the traditional cuisine and street foods. Being immunized can give you peace of mind while traveling because hepatitis A is spread by tainted food and water.

Hepatitis B: Take into account the Hepatitis B vaccine for extended visits, close contact with locals, or any medical operations.

Body fluids are the primary means of transmission, and the vaccine can offer long-lasting protection.

Typhoid: As this bacterial infection can be caught by contaminated food and water, a typhoid vaccine is something to think about if you plan to eat from street sellers or travel to more rural areas.

As rabies can be present in some local species, see a healthcare professional about the rabies vaccine if you intend to engage in outdoor activities, go trekking, or interact with animals.

To make sure you have enough time to complete any required vaccinations, it's crucial to speak with a travel health specialist or your healthcare practitioner at least 4-6 weeks before your trip. Do not forget to take additional protective steps, such as wearing insect repellent to avoid getting sick from mosquitoes.

Dealing with Emergencies

In Granada, handling crises calls for a combination of readiness, fast thinking, and having access to the right tools. Even though they are unplanned, understanding how to react in an emergency will ensure your safety and well-being. Here are some crucial pointers for handling crises in Granada:

Know the Emergency Numbers: Become familiar with the Spanish emergency phone numbers. You can reach police, emergency medical services, and fire departments by dialing 112, which is the universal emergency number. Don't forget to save and keep this phone number handy.

Get Help Right Away: In the event of a medical emergency, get help right away by contacting an ambulance or going to the closest hospital. Although Spanish healthcare institutions offer high-quality care, it can be helpful to get travel insurance that includes medical emergencies.

English is frequently spoken in tourist destinations, but knowing a few basic Spanish words can help you communicate in an emergency. Don't be afraid to approach locals or the staff at your accommodation for help if necessary.

Consult your country's embassy or consulate in Spain for assistance and direction if you experience a serious emergency, such as the loss of crucial documents or legal problems.

In instances like natural catastrophes or civil emergencies, pay attention to and abide by the directions of local authorities. They will offer instructions on safety precautions and evacuation protocols.

Keep Up-to-Date With Local News and Weather Reports: Stay informed, especially if you have outdoor plans or it's raining or storming outside.

Consider registering with the embassy or consulate of your native country using their travel registration service. This makes it easier for them to contact you in an emergency or to provide you with pertinent travel advice.

Carry Important Papers Securely: Keep backup copies of your identity, travel papers, and emergency contact information in a safe and secure location.

Although making decisions in an emergency can be difficult, maintaining your composure will help. Like many towns, Granada places a high priority on safety, thus asking for help from locals or other travelers is always recommended. You may enjoy your time in Granada with assurance knowing that you are ready to manage any unexpected issue that may happen by being organized and alert.

Conclusion

As we reach the end of **The Ultimate Granada Travel Guide,** we hope this journey through the heart of Andalusia has filled your soul with the magic and allure of this extraordinary city. Granada, with its intricate tapestry of history, culture, and natural wonders, leaves an indelible mark on all who wander its enchanting streets.

We have walked in the footsteps of kings within the walls of the Alhambra, marveling at its timeless beauty and the whispers of its storied past. We have wandered through the ancient maze of Albayzín, where the echoes of bygone eras resonate in the soul-stirring melodies of flamenco and the vibrant artistry of its people.

Beyond the grandeur of its historical landmarks, Granada beckoned us to savor the simple joys of life - the delightful cacophony of a bustling market, the camaraderie of sharing tapas with newfound friends, and the warmth of the locals' hospitality, embracing us as one of their own.

Venturing into the embrace of nature, we discovered the awe-inspiring landscapes of the Sierra Nevada, where snow-capped peaks stand tall against cerulean skies, and the Alpujarras' picturesque villages stand as testaments to the resilience of time-honored traditions.

As we immersed ourselves in the heartbeat of Granada's culture, we learned that this city is more than just a destination; it's an experience that ignites a passion for life and leaves us forever connected to the beauty of human expression and creativity.

Our ultimate Granada Travel Guide has aimed to be your trusted companion, providing you with the tools to craft your unique adventure, unearth hidden gems, and embrace the diversity and authenticity that makes this city so special.

As you bid farewell to Granada, may your heart be filled with cherished memories, and your spirit be forever intertwined with the vibrant spirit of this Andalusian jewel. Carry with you the echoes of flamenco rhythms, the taste of delectable tapas, and the vivid colors of Granada's landscapes.

Remember, Granada, will forever await your return, ready to reveal new secrets and create more unforgettable moments. So, until we meet again, keep the spirit of Granada alive in your heart, and let the magic of this city inspire your future travels and adventures.

Safe journeys, dear explorer, and may the enchantment of Granada accompany you wherever your next destination may be. The world is vast, and the wonders it holds are endless.

As we conclude this chapter, remember that the spirit of exploration and discovery will forever guide you on the path to new horizons.

Thank you for choosing **The Ultimate Granada Travel Guide**, and may your travels be filled with joy, enlightenment, and the timeless allure of wanderlust. Farewell, and may your next adventure be even more wondrous than the last!

Printed in Great Britain
by Amazon